Mastering SD A Comprehensive Gu Defined Wide Area Networking

CW00495221

Table of Contents:

Chapter 1: Introduction to SD-WAN

In today's rapidly evolving digital landscape, where organizations are increasingly relying on cloud-based applications, remote offices, and mobile workers, the traditional Wide Area Network (WAN) infrastructure is facing significant challenges. As demands for greater bandwidth, improved performance, and enhanced security grow, a revolutionary networking paradigm has emerged – Software-Defined Wide Area Networking (SD-WAN). This chapter delves into the foundational aspects of SD-WAN, tracing its origins, elucidating its benefits, and unveiling the core components that make up its architecture.

1.1 What is SD-WAN?

SD-WAN, an acronym for Software-Defined Wide Area Networking, is a transformative networking technology that leverages software-defined principles to optimize and manage Wide Area Network connections. Unlike traditional WAN setups that often rely on rigid, hardware-based configurations, SD-WAN offers a dynamic and flexible approach by abstracting network control from underlying hardware. This abstraction enables organizations to centrally manage and control their network traffic through software-defined policies, enhancing visibility, agility, and efficiency.

At its core, SD-WAN augments traditional WAN connections by incorporating various transport technologies, including Multiprotocol Label Switching (MPLS), broadband internet, and even cellular networks, into a unified and intelligent network architecture. By intelligently routing traffic based on application requirements, network conditions, and security policies, SD-WAN optimizes application performance while maintaining security and reliability.

1.2 Evolution of Wide Area Networking

To understand the significance of SD-WAN, it is essential to trace the evolution of Wide Area Networking. Traditional WANs primarily relied on private dedicated circuits, often MPLS, to connect remote sites to a central data center. While MPLS provided a high level of security and reliability, it came with limitations such as high costs, limited bandwidth, and slow provisioning times.

The rise of cloud computing and the proliferation of bandwidth-intensive applications, such as video conferencing and real-time collaboration tools, strained traditional WAN architectures. This led to the development of hybrid WANs, combining MPLS with cheaper broadband connections. However, managing and optimizing traffic across such hybrid setups became increasingly complex.

Enter SD-WAN, which builds upon the foundation of hybrid WANs while introducing dynamic path selection, application-aware routing, and centralized management. SD-WAN's ability to seamlessly integrate multiple transport options and prioritize traffic based on business needs addresses the shortcomings of traditional WAN setups, paving the way for a more agile and responsive networking solution.

1.3 Benefits and Use Cases of SD-WAN

The adoption of SD-WAN offers a plethora of benefits that directly address the challenges faced by conventional WAN architectures. Some of the key advantages include:

- **Enhanced Performance:** SD-WAN's intelligent traffic routing and optimization ensure that critical applications receive the necessary bandwidth and low-latency paths, leading to improved user experiences.

- **Cost Efficiency:** By incorporating cost-effective broadband connections alongside MPLS, organizations can significantly reduce network expenses without compromising performance.

- **Agility and Flexibility:** SD-WAN's software-defined nature allows for rapid deployment and simplified configuration changes, enabling IT teams to adapt quickly to changing business requirements.

- **Security:** SD-WAN integrates security features such as encryption, firewall capabilities, and threat detection, ensuring that data remains protected across the network.

- **Centralized Management:** The centralized orchestration and management of SD-WAN simplify network administration, policy enforcement, and monitoring, regardless of the geographical distribution of sites.

Use cases for SD-WAN span various industries and scenarios, including:

- **Branch Office Connectivity:** SD-WAN enables efficient and secure connectivity between branch offices and the central data center, enhancing application performance and reducing the need for costly dedicated lines.

- **Cloud Connectivity:** Organizations can seamlessly connect to cloud resources, optimizing the performance of cloud-based applications while maintaining security and control.

- **Mobile Workforce:** SD-WAN ensures consistent and secure connectivity for remote and mobile workers, whether they are accessing resources from corporate headquarters or on the go.

1.4 Key Components of SD-WAN Architecture

SD-WAN's architecture is composed of several fundamental components that work in concert to deliver its capabilities:

- **Edge Devices and Gateways:** These devices, often located at branch offices or remote sites, establish connections to the

WAN and perform traffic management tasks based on predefined policies.

- **Orchestrators and Controllers:** Centralized management platforms that define, enforce, and modify network policies, ensuring consistent and optimized traffic routing across the network.

- **Overlay and Underlay Networks:** The overlay network abstracts the underlying transport technologies, while the underlay network consists of the physical connections, such as MPLS and broadband, that transport the data.

- **Security Integration:** SD-WAN incorporates security features, such as encryption and firewalls, to safeguard data and applications as they traverse the network.

This chapter has provided a comprehensive overview of SD-WAN, introducing its core concepts, evolution, benefits, and key architectural components. In the chapters that follow, we will delve deeper into the intricacies of SD-WAN, exploring its underlying technologies, deployment models, routing mechanisms, security measures, and real-world case studies, empowering readers to master the art of Software-Defined Wide Area Networking.

Chapter 2: Underlying Technologies

In the realm of Software-Defined Wide Area Networking (SD-WAN), a profound shift in underlying technologies has taken place, reshaping the way networks are designed, managed, and optimized. This chapter explores the technological foundations that underpin SD-WAN's capabilities, including the challenges posed by traditional WAN approaches, the concepts of overlay and underlay networks, the role of virtualization and Network Functions Virtualization (NFV), and the critical importance of Quality of Service (QoS) and traffic management.

2.1 MPLS vs. Internet: Traditional WAN Challenges

Traditional WAN architectures, often reliant on Multiprotocol Label Switching (MPLS), presented a set of challenges as networks evolved to accommodate new demands. MPLS provided a secure and reliable connection but came with limitations, including:

- **Cost:** MPLS circuits were expensive to provision and maintain, particularly for organizations with multiple remote sites.

- **Scalability:** As businesses expanded, adding new sites, or increasing bandwidth often required time-consuming and costly adjustments.

- **Latency and Performance:** MPLS connections, while reliable, didn't always offer optimal performance for latency-sensitive applications.

- **Complexity:** Managing diverse connections, such as MPLS, broadband, and cellular, introduced complexity and made traffic optimization cumbersome.

The emergence of SD-WAN addressed these challenges by enabling organizations to intelligently route traffic based on real-time conditions, application priorities, and security requirements.

2.2 Overlay and Underlay Networks

At the heart of SD-WAN architecture lies the concept of overlay and underlay networks. The overlay network abstracts the physical underlay network, enabling the creation of a logical, virtualized network on top of existing infrastructure. This overlay approach provides several benefits:

- **Flexibility:** Overlay networks enable the use of multiple transport technologies, such as MPLS, broadband, and LTE, without the need to modify the underlying physical infrastructure.

- **Traffic Optimization:** SD-WAN's overlay intelligently routes traffic based on real-time conditions, optimizing performance and reliability.

- **Simplified Management:** By decoupling the logical network from the physical infrastructure, centralized management and policy enforcement become more streamlined.

2.3 Virtualization and Network Functions Virtualization (NFV)

Virtualization is a core principle underlying SD-WAN's agility and flexibility. By abstracting network functions from dedicated hardware, SD-WAN leverages Network Functions Virtualization (NFV) to create a dynamic and adaptable network environment. Key aspects of NFV in SD-WAN include:

- **Virtual Edge Devices:** SD-WAN leverages virtual edge devices that can be instantiated on commodity hardware or as virtual machines. This virtualization enhances scalability and reduces hardware dependencies.

- **Service Chaining:** NFV allows for the chaining of network functions, such as routing, firewalling, and WAN optimization, in a virtualized environment, enabling efficient traffic flow and security enforcement.

- **Rapid Deployment:** Virtualized components can be provisioned quickly and remotely, reducing deployment times, and enabling organizations to respond swiftly to changing network requirements.

2.4 Quality of Service (QoS) and Traffic Management

In the modern networking landscape, ensuring consistent application performance and user experiences is paramount. Quality of Service (QoS) mechanisms in SD-WAN play a pivotal role in achieving this goal:

- **Application-Aware Routing:** SD-WAN employs deep packet inspection and application identification to intelligently route traffic based on application priorities and network conditions.

- **Dynamic Path Selection:** SD-WAN dynamically selects the optimal path for traffic based on factors like latency, jitter, and packet loss, ensuring optimal performance.

- **Traffic Shaping and Prioritization:** QoS policies enable the allocation of bandwidth and the prioritization of critical applications over less essential traffic.

- **Real-Time Monitoring:** SD-WAN continuously monitors network performance and application behavior, allowing for real-time adjustments to QoS policies and traffic management.

By effectively managing traffic, QoS, and application performance, SD-WAN enhances the user experience, accelerates application delivery, and optimizes network resources.

In this chapter, we've delved into the foundational technologies that enable the transformational capabilities of SD-WAN. From overlay and underlay networks to the role of virtualization and NFV, as well as the critical importance of Quality of Service and traffic management, these technologies form the bedrock upon which SD-WAN's innovation is built. In the chapters ahead, we will explore the intricacies of SD-WAN's architecture, deployment models, security integration, and real-world applications, empowering readers to navigate the dynamic landscape of Software-Defined Wide Area Networking.

Chapter 3: SD-WAN Architecture

The architectural design of Software-Defined Wide Area Networking (SD-WAN) is a critical factor in its ability to revolutionize network connectivity. This chapter delves deep into the intricacies of SD-WAN's architecture, exploring the pivotal choices between centralized and distributed control planes, the role of edge devices and gateways, the orchestration and control provided by orchestrators and controllers, and the imperative integration of security measures within the SD-WAN framework.

3.1 Centralized vs. Distributed Control Plane

A fundamental decision in SD-WAN architecture revolves around the control plane – the brain of the network that determines how data traffic is managed and routed. SD-WAN offers two primary models:

- **Centralized Control Plane:** In this model, a central orchestrator or controller exercises control over the entire network, making decisions on traffic routing, QoS policies, and security measures. Centralization provides a unified management interface, simplifying network administration, policy enforcement, and monitoring.

- **Distributed Control Plane:** Here, edge devices and gateways play a more active role in traffic management, making localized routing decisions based on predefined policies. This approach offers faster decision-making and the ability to adapt to real-time network conditions at the edge.

The choice between centralized and distributed control planes hinges on factors such as network size, complexity, and the need for real-time responsiveness.

11

3.2 Edge Devices and Gateways

At the network's edge, edge devices and gateways are key components that play a pivotal role in SD-WAN architecture. These devices provide the interface between the local network and the wider SD-WAN environment. Their functions include:

- **Traffic Routing:** Edge devices route traffic based on policies set by the central control plane or distributed intelligence.

- **Application Visibility:** They perform deep packet inspection to identify applications and apply QoS and security policies accordingly.

- **Path Selection:** Edge devices select the optimal path for traffic based on network conditions, performance requirements, and application priorities.

- **Security:** Gateways often integrate security features like firewalls, intrusion detection, and encryption to safeguard data as it traverses the network.

3.3 Orchestrators and Controllers

The orchestration and control layers are the command centers of SD-WAN architecture. Orchestrators and controllers provide:

- **Policy Definition:** Orchestrators define policies that dictate how traffic is managed, prioritized, and routed across the network.

- **Centralized Management:** Controllers enforce policies, monitor network health, and optimize traffic flows across the SD-WAN infrastructure.

- **Real-Time Adaptability:** Controllers continuously assess network conditions and adjust routing decisions to ensure optimal performance and application delivery.

- **Scalability:** Orchestrators and controllers enable network-wide management, making it easier to scale SD-WAN deployments as the organization grows.

3.4 Security Integration in SD-WAN

In the modern digital landscape, security is paramount. SD-WAN's architecture recognizes this by integrating security measures directly into its design:

- **Encryption:** SD-WAN encrypts data traffic, protecting it from unauthorized access and ensuring the confidentiality of sensitive information.

- **Firewall Integration:** Many SD-WAN solutions incorporate firewall capabilities at the edge, enhancing security by inspecting and filtering traffic.

- **Intrusion Detection and Prevention:** SD-WAN can detect and prevent intrusion attempts, blocking malicious traffic before it enters the network.

- **Secure Web Gateways:** Some SD-WAN solutions offer integrated secure web gateways to protect against web-based threats and ensure safe internet access.

By seamlessly weaving security into its architecture, SD-WAN ensures that data and applications remain protected as they traverse the network.

In this chapter, we have delved into the intricacies of SD-WAN architecture, examining the choices between centralized and distributed control planes, the role of edge devices and gateways, the importance of orchestrators and controllers, and the integration of security measures. This understanding forms a crucial foundation as we progress through the book, exploring topics such as deployment models, routing mechanisms, security strategies, and real-world implementations of Software-Defined Wide Area Networking.

Chapter 4: Deployment Models

Deploying a Software-Defined Wide Area Networking (SD-WAN) solution is a strategic endeavor that can reshape an organization's network infrastructure. This chapter explores various deployment models, each tailored to address specific business needs and challenges. We will delve into the nuances of on-premises SD-WAN, cloud-delivered SD-WAN, hybrid deployments, and the advantages offered by managed SD-WAN services.

4.1 On-Premises SD-WAN

On-Premises SD-WAN refers to deploying SD-WAN technology within an organization's own data centers or branch offices. In this model:

- **Control and Flexibility:** Organizations retain full control over their SD-WAN deployment, allowing for customization and adaptation to specific network requirements.

- **Data Security:** On-premises SD-WAN can offer heightened data security, particularly for sensitive applications and industries with strict compliance requirements.

- **Latency Control:** For latency-sensitive applications, on-premises deployment ensures minimal delay by keeping data traffic within the organization's local infrastructure.

- **Initial Investment:** Organizations must invest in hardware, software licenses, and maintenance, which can incur higher upfront costs.

4.2 Cloud-Delivered SD-WAN

Cloud-Delivered SD-WAN moves the control and management of the network to the cloud, with edge devices connecting to cloud-based controllers. Key features of this deployment model include:

- **Scalability:** Cloud-delivered SD-WAN offers seamless scalability, enabling organizations to quickly expand or contract their network as needed.

- **Reduced Hardware Overhead:** Organizations benefit from reduced hardware costs, as controllers and management components are hosted in the cloud.

- **Centralized Management:** Cloud-based controllers provide centralized visibility and management across distributed locations.

- **Latency Considerations:** Depending on the location of cloud resources and data centers, latency for some applications may vary.

4.3 Hybrid SD-WAN Deployments

Hybrid SD-WAN deployments blend the best of both on-premises and cloud-delivered models, combining localized control with the flexibility of the cloud:

- **Optimized Performance:** Hybrid deployments allow organizations to route latency-sensitive traffic through on-premises SD-WAN while offloading non-sensitive traffic to the cloud.

- **Cost Efficiency:** Organizations can leverage cost-effective cloud connections for non-critical traffic, reducing the reliance on more expensive dedicated circuits.

- **Application Prioritization:** Hybrid deployments enable fine-grained control over application routing, ensuring optimal performance and user experiences.

4.4 Managed SD-WAN Services

Managed SD-WAN services involve partnering with a third-party provider to handle various aspects of SD-WAN deployment and management:

- **Expertise and Support:** Managed services offer access to skilled professionals who handle deployment, configuration, and ongoing management of the SD-WAN infrastructure.

- **Resource Offloading:** Organizations can focus on core business activities while leaving the technical intricacies of SD-WAN to the managed service provider.

- **Cost Predictability:** Managed services often offer predictable monthly costs, helping organizations manage their budgets more effectively.

- **Vendor Selection:** Choosing a reliable managed service provider is crucial to ensure a successful SD-WAN deployment.

By exploring these deployment models – on-premises, cloud-delivered, hybrid, and managed services – organizations can make informed decisions that align with their business goals and network requirements. In the following chapters, we will delve into the technical aspects of SD-WAN, including routing mechanisms, security integration, and real-world case studies, empowering readers to implement and optimize SD-WAN solutions tailored to their specific needs.

Chapter 5: SD-WAN Routing and Traffic Steering

The heart of Software-Defined Wide Area Networking (SD-WAN) lies in its ability to intelligently route and manage network traffic, ensuring optimal performance, reliability, and security. This chapter explores the intricacies of SD-WAN routing and traffic steering, shedding light on dynamic path selection, application-aware routing, load balancing, failover mechanisms, and the streamlined efficiency of zero-touch provisioning.

5.1 Dynamic Path Selection

Dynamic path selection is a core capability of SD-WAN that enables the real-time optimization of traffic routing based on network conditions, application requirements, and performance metrics. Key aspects of dynamic path selection include:

- **Path Metrics:** SD-WAN continuously measures parameters such as latency, jitter, packet loss, and bandwidth availability across multiple paths.

- **Policy-Based Routing:** Policies define how traffic should be routed based on predetermined criteria, ensuring that specific applications or data types take priority.

- **Real-Time Adaptation:** SD-WAN dynamically adjusts traffic routing based on changing network conditions to maintain optimal performance.

5.2 Application-Aware Routing

Traditional routing treats all network traffic equally, regardless of the type of application generating it. SD-WAN's application-aware routing brings intelligence to the routing process by considering the unique requirements of each application:

- **Deep Packet Inspection:** SD-WAN devices identify applications within network traffic packets, enabling accurate application classification.

- **QoS Differentiation:** Applications are prioritized based on their criticality, ensuring that latency-sensitive applications receive the necessary bandwidth and resources.

- **Policy-Driven Routing:** Policies dictate how specific applications are routed, allowing organizations to align routing decisions with business objectives.

5.3 Load Balancing and Failover

Load balancing and failover mechanisms play a crucial role in maintaining network resiliency and optimal performance:

- **Traffic Distribution:** Load balancing distributes traffic across multiple paths to prevent congestion and utilize available bandwidth effectively.

- **Link Failover:** When a network link experiences issues, SD-WAN can automatically reroute traffic to a healthier path, minimizing disruptions.

- **Link Aggregation:** SD-WAN can aggregate multiple links to create a higher bandwidth connection, enhancing overall network capacity.

5.4 Zero-Touch Provisioning

Zero-Touch Provisioning (ZTP) streamlines the deployment process, enabling rapid and consistent setup of SD-WAN devices:

- **Automated Configuration:** Devices are pre-configured with provisioning templates, enabling automatic setup when connected to the network.

- **Remote Deployment:** SD-WAN devices can be shipped to remote locations, reducing the need for on-site technical expertise.

- **Consistency and Scalability:** ZTP ensures uniform device configurations and simplifies the process of deploying and managing large numbers of devices.

By leveraging dynamic path selection, application-aware routing, load balancing, failover mechanisms, and zero-touch provisioning, SD-WAN transforms the way networks handle traffic, ensuring optimized performance, resiliency, and operational efficiency. As we progress through this comprehensive guide, we will delve further into the multifaceted aspects of SD-WAN, including security integration, management, real-world implementations, and emerging trends, empowering readers to harness the full potential of Software-Defined Wide Area Networking.

Chapter 6: Security in SD-WAN

In an era of heightened cyber threats and data breaches, ensuring robust security measures is paramount in every networking solution. Software-Defined Wide Area Networking (SD-WAN) not only enhances connectivity and performance but also introduces innovative security features to safeguard network traffic and data. This chapter delves into the comprehensive security aspects of SD-WAN, covering encryption, firewall integration, intrusion detection and prevention, and the role of secure web gateways.

6.1 Encryption and Data Privacy

Encryption serves as the cornerstone of data protection in SD-WAN. By encrypting data traffic as it traverses the network, SD-WAN ensures that sensitive information remains confidential, even in the event of unauthorized interception. Key aspects of encryption and data privacy in SD-WAN include:

- **End-to-End Encryption:** SD-WAN employs encryption protocols to secure data from source to destination, guarding against eavesdropping and unauthorized access.

- **Data Integrity:** Encryption prevents data tampering during transmission, maintaining the integrity of information exchanged between endpoints.

- **Compliance:** Encryption measures in SD-WAN help organizations adhere to regulatory requirements and data privacy standards.

6.2 Firewall Integration

Integrating firewall capabilities within SD-WAN architecture bolsters network security by filtering and inspecting traffic at the network edge:

- **Intrusion Prevention:** Firewalls in SD-WAN can identify and block suspicious traffic patterns, mitigating potential intrusion attempts.

- **Application Control:** Firewalls classify, and control traffic based on application signatures, preventing unauthorized or malicious applications from accessing the network.

- **Granular Policies:** SD-WAN firewalls enable fine-grained policy enforcement, allowing organizations to customize security measures for different applications and users.

6.3 Intrusion Detection and Prevention

SD-WAN's intrusion detection and prevention mechanisms contribute to a proactive approach to network security:

- **Anomaly Detection:** SD-WAN devices monitor network traffic patterns and behaviors to identify deviations that may indicate intrusion attempts.

- **Real-Time Response:** Upon detecting suspicious activity, SD-WAN can take immediate action, such as blocking or rerouting traffic to prevent potential threats.

- **Signature-Based Detection:** Intrusion detection and prevention systems use known attack signatures to identify and thwart known threats.

6.4 Secure Web Gateways

Secure web gateways in SD-WAN provide a robust defense against web-based threats and ensure safe internet access:

- **URL Filtering:** SD-WAN gateways filter web traffic based on URL categories, blocking access to malicious or inappropriate websites.

- **Malware Protection:** Gateways scan web content for malware and prevent users from inadvertently downloading malicious files.

- **Cloud Application Security:** SD-WAN gateways can inspect and control access to cloud-based applications, ensuring secure usage of SaaS platforms.

By addressing encryption, firewall integration, intrusion detection and prevention, and secure web gateways, SD-WAN establishes a comprehensive security framework that safeguards network traffic and data. As we delve deeper into this comprehensive guide, we will continue to explore the multifaceted aspects of SD-WAN, including performance optimization, management, real-world implementations, and emerging trends, empowering readers to navigate the intricacies of Software-Defined Wide Area Networking with confidence.

Chapter 7: Performance Optimization and QoS

Achieving optimal network performance and Quality of Service (QoS) is a primary objective of any network deployment. Software-Defined Wide Area Networking (SD-WAN) not only enhances connectivity but also offers an array of tools and techniques to optimize performance and ensure consistent application experiences. This chapter explores the intricacies of performance optimization and QoS in SD-WAN, encompassing WAN optimization techniques, bandwidth aggregation, traffic shaping, prioritization, and real-time application performance monitoring.

7.1 WAN Optimization Techniques

WAN optimization techniques in SD-WAN are designed to improve the efficiency of data transmission and minimize latency:

- **Data Compression:** SD-WAN compresses data before transmission, reducing the volume of traffic and enhancing overall throughput.

- **Data Deduplication:** Redundant data is identified and removed before transmission, minimizing the amount of data sent across the network.

- **Protocol Optimization:** SD-WAN optimizes the behavior of network protocols, reducing protocol overhead and improving efficiency.

7.2 Bandwidth Aggregation and Link Bonding

Bandwidth aggregation and link bonding combine multiple network links to create a single, higher-capacity connection:

- **Link Load Balancing:** SD-WAN balances traffic across multiple links to utilize available bandwidth effectively and prevent congestion.

- **Link Bonding:** Multiple links are combined to create a single logical connection, increasing overall bandwidth and network capacity.

- **Dynamic Path Selection:** SD-WAN intelligently routes traffic across different links based on real-time network conditions, ensuring optimal performance.

7.3 Traffic Shaping and Prioritization

Traffic shaping and prioritization mechanisms enable organizations to allocate network resources based on application requirements:

- **Quality of Service (QoS):** SD-WAN assigns priority levels to different types of traffic, ensuring that critical applications receive the necessary bandwidth and resources.

- **Application Steering:** Traffic is directed along specific paths based on application requirements, optimizing performance and user experiences.

- **Path Selection Policies:** Organizations can define policies that dictate how traffic is routed and prioritized, aligning with business objectives.

7.4 Real-Time Application Performance Monitoring

Real-time application performance monitoring provides actionable insights into network behavior and application responsiveness:

- **Network Visibility:** SD-WAN solutions offer visibility into network performance, allowing organizations to identify and address potential bottlenecks or issues.

- **Proactive Issue Resolution:** Real-time monitoring enables organizations to identify performance degradation or anomalies and take proactive measures to rectify them.

- **User Experience Optimization:** By closely monitoring application performance, SD-WAN helps ensure a consistent and positive user experience for remote and branch users.

By leveraging WAN optimization techniques, bandwidth aggregation, traffic shaping, prioritization, and real-time application performance monitoring, SD-WAN empowers organizations to unlock the full potential of their network infrastructure. As we delve further into this comprehensive guide, we will continue to explore the multifaceted aspects of SD-WAN, including management, real-world implementations, security strategies, and emerging trends, equipping readers with the knowledge and tools to master the intricacies of Software-Defined Wide Area Networking.

Chapter 8: Managing and Monitoring SD-WAN

Effectively managing and monitoring a Software-Defined Wide Area Networking (SD-WAN) deployment is essential for maintaining network performance, security, and operational efficiency. This chapter delves into the critical aspects of managing and monitoring SD-WAN, covering configuration and policy management, network health and performance monitoring, troubleshooting and diagnostics, and the value of analytics and reporting.

8.1 Configuration and Policy Management

Configuration and policy management form the foundation of SD-WAN administration, enabling organizations to define how network traffic is handled:

- **Centralized Control:** SD-WAN solutions offer a centralized interface for configuring and managing network policies across multiple locations.

- **Policy Definition:** Organizations can define policies that dictate how applications are routed, prioritized, and secured across the network.

- **Change Management:** SD-WAN solutions streamline the process of making configuration changes and applying policy updates across the network.

8.2 Monitoring Network Health and Performance

Continuous monitoring of network health and performance is crucial to maintaining optimal operation and identifying potential issues:

- **Real-Time Monitoring:** SD-WAN provides real-time visibility into network conditions, allowing organizations to detect and address anomalies promptly.

- **Performance Metrics:** SD-WAN monitors parameters such as latency, jitter, packet loss, and bandwidth utilization, providing insights into network quality.

- **Alerting and Notifications:** Automated alerts and notifications inform IT teams of performance degradation or critical events, enabling rapid response.

8.3 Troubleshooting and Diagnostics

Rapid identification and resolution of network issues are essential for minimizing downtime and ensuring consistent user experiences:

- **Root Cause Analysis:** SD-WAN solutions offer tools for diagnosing and identifying the root causes of network performance problems.

- **Path Testing:** Troubleshooting features enable IT teams to simulate traffic paths, diagnose issues, and validate the effectiveness of configuration changes.

- **Remote Remediation:** Troubleshooting and diagnostic capabilities can often be performed remotely, reducing the need for on-site intervention.

8.4 Analytics and Reporting

Data-driven insights provided by SD-WAN analytics and reporting play a vital role in optimizing network performance and making informed decisions:

- **Trend Analysis:** Analyzing historical data allows organizations to identify patterns, make capacity planning decisions, and anticipate network requirements.

- **User Behavior:** SD-WAN analytics can shed light on user behavior, helping organizations optimize application delivery and QoS policies.

- **Compliance and Auditing:** Detailed reporting supports compliance efforts by providing audit trails and data on network activities.

By effectively managing and monitoring SD-WAN deployments through configuration and policy management, network health and performance monitoring, troubleshooting and diagnostics, and analytics and reporting, organizations can ensure a resilient, secure, and high-performing network infrastructure. As we progress through this comprehensive guide, we will continue to explore the multifaceted aspects of SD-WAN, including security integration, real-world implementations, emerging trends, and best practices, empowering readers to master the art of Software-Defined Wide Area Networking.

Chapter 9: SD-WAN and Cloud Services

The integration of cloud services into modern business operations has transformed the way organizations operate and deliver services. Software-Defined Wide Area Networking (SD-WAN) plays a pivotal role in ensuring seamless and optimized connectivity to cloud resources. This chapter explores the synergy between SD-WAN and cloud services, addressing cloud connectivity challenges, the choice between direct cloud access and backhauling, multi-cloud connectivity, and strategies for optimizing Software-as-a-Service (SaaS) application performance.

9.1 Cloud Connectivity Challenges

The shift to cloud services introduces unique challenges related to connectivity, performance, and security:

- **Latency and Performance:** Traditional WAN architectures may introduce latency when accessing cloud resources, impacting application responsiveness.

- **Security:** Ensuring consistent security measures across the WAN while connecting to diverse cloud environments is crucial.

- **Complexity:** Managing multiple cloud connections and ensuring consistent application performance can be complex and resource intensive.

9.2 Direct Cloud Access vs. Backhauling

SD-WAN offers two primary approaches to connecting to cloud resources: direct cloud access and backhauling:

- **Direct Cloud Access:** SD-WAN enables branch offices to connect directly to cloud resources, reducing latency and improving application performance.

- **Backhauling:** Traffic is routed through the central data center before reaching the cloud, allowing for consistent security policies but potentially introducing latency.

9.3 Multi-Cloud Connectivity

Many organizations adopt multi-cloud strategies to leverage multiple cloud providers for different purposes:

- **Vendor Diversity:** Multi-cloud environments offer vendor diversity, reducing dependency on a single provider.

- **Optimized Performance:** SD-WAN enables efficient and secure connectivity to multiple cloud environments, optimizing application performance.

- **Dynamic Path Selection:** SD-WAN dynamically selects the best path for traffic to each cloud provider based on real-time conditions.

9.4 Optimizing SaaS Application Performance

SD-WAN offers strategies to enhance the performance of SaaS applications:

- **Path Optimization:** SD-WAN can identify and route SaaS traffic through the optimal path to minimize latency.

- **Application Steering:** SaaS-aware routing ensures that SaaS traffic is directed along the most suitable path based on performance requirements.

- **QoS Policies:** SD-WAN assigns higher priority to SaaS traffic, ensuring that critical applications receive the necessary bandwidth.

By seamlessly integrating with cloud services and addressing challenges such as cloud connectivity, direct cloud access, multi-cloud connectivity, and SaaS application performance optimization,

SD-WAN enhances the efficiency, reliability, and agility of network connectivity. As we journey through this comprehensive guide, we will continue to explore the multifaceted aspects of SD-WAN, including real-world implementations, security strategies, emerging trends, and best practices, empowering readers to navigate the dynamic landscape of Software-Defined Wide Area Networking with confidence.

Chapter 10: Case Studies and Real-World Implementations

The true testament of a technology's value lies in its real-world applications. In this chapter, we delve into case studies that highlight the transformative impact of Software-Defined Wide Area Networking (SD-WAN) across various industries. From retail to financial services, healthcare to manufacturing, SD-WAN showcases its versatility and ability to address diverse challenges. These case studies shed light on how SD-WAN has enabled branch network transformation, provided secure and compliant connectivity, facilitated telemedicine and remote clinics, and optimized global supply chain management.

10.1 Retail Industry: Branch Network Transformation

Challenge: A retail chain with numerous branches faced connectivity issues, slow application performance, and difficulty in managing network policies across locations.

Solution: SD-WAN was deployed to streamline network connectivity, optimize traffic routing, and enhance application performance. Centralized policy management allowed for consistent application prioritization and security measures across all branches.

Outcome: The retail chain experienced improved application responsiveness, efficient management of network policies, and reduced downtime. The ability to scale and adapt to changing network requirements enabled seamless expansion and enhanced customer experiences.

10.2 Financial Services: Secure and Compliant Connectivity

Challenge: A financial services organization needed to ensure secure communication across its branches while adhering to stringent compliance regulations.

Solution: SD-WAN was implemented to encrypt data traffic, provide firewall integration, and enable intrusion detection and prevention. Dynamic path selection ensured optimal performance, while secure web gateways protected against web-based threats.

Outcome: The financial services firm achieved robust security and compliance, maintaining the confidentiality of sensitive financial data. SD-WAN's flexibility allowed for quick adjustments to security policies and ensured continuous compliance with evolving regulations.

10.3 Healthcare: Telemedicine and Remote Clinics

Challenge: A healthcare provider sought to extend its services to remote clinics and enable telemedicine consultations, requiring reliable connectivity and real-time communication.

Solution: SD-WAN facilitated direct cloud access for telemedicine applications, optimizing performance and reducing latency. QoS policies ensured high-quality video conferencing, while failover mechanisms guaranteed uninterrupted communication.

Outcome: The healthcare provider successfully expanded its reach to remote clinics, enhancing patient care through telemedicine services. SD-WAN's ability to ensure seamless connectivity and reliable performance supported the delivery of critical healthcare services.

10.4 Manufacturing: Global Supply Chain Management

Challenge: A manufacturing company with a complex global supply chain needed efficient communication and data exchange between its production facilities and suppliers.

Solution: SD-WAN enabled bandwidth aggregation, optimizing data transfer between manufacturing sites and suppliers. Application-aware routing ensured timely and reliable delivery of production data and inventory information.

Outcome: The manufacturing company achieved enhanced supply chain efficiency, enabling real-time collaboration, data sharing, and production coordination. SD-WAN's optimization capabilities supported smoother operations and reduced lead times.

These real-world case studies underscore the transformative impact of SD-WAN across diverse industries, showcasing its ability to address specific challenges and deliver tangible benefits. As we conclude this comprehensive guide, we have explored the intricacies of Software-Defined Wide Area Networking, including its architecture, deployment models, security integration, performance optimization, cloud connectivity, and real-world implementations. Armed with this knowledge, readers are equipped to navigate the complexities of SD-WAN and leverage its capabilities to unlock new possibilities in the world of networking and connectivity.

Chapter 11: Future Trends and Emerging Technologies

As the technology landscape continues to evolve, Software-Defined Wide Area Networking (SD-WAN) stands at the forefront of innovation, shaping the future of networking and connectivity. In this chapter, we explore the exciting realm of future trends and emerging technologies that are set to redefine the capabilities and potential of SD-WAN. From the integration of Artificial Intelligence (AI) and Machine Learning to the evolution of the SD-WAN ecosystem, we delve into Secure Access Service Edge (SASE), and the transformative impact of 5G and Edge Computing integration.

11.1 AI and Machine Learning in SD-WAN

AI and Machine Learning are poised to revolutionize SD-WAN by enhancing automation, decision-making, and network intelligence:

- **Predictive Analytics:** AI-driven algorithms can predict network anomalies and performance issues, enabling proactive mitigation.

- **Dynamic Path Optimization:** Machine Learning algorithms can adaptively optimize traffic routing based on real-time conditions, ensuring optimal performance.

- **Security Enhancement:** AI can detect and respond to security threats in real time, fortifying SD-WAN's defense against cyberattacks.

11.2 Secure Access Service Edge (SASE)

Secure Access Service Edge (SASE) is a transformative architectural framework that integrates networking and security into a unified cloud-based model:

- **Converged Services:** SASE combines SD-WAN and security functions, delivering comprehensive protection and connectivity.

- **Edge-Centric Approach:** SASE shifts security and networking services to the edge of the network, providing secure access for users, devices, and applications.

- **Cloud-Native Architecture:** SASE leverages cloud-based resources to deliver scalable, flexible, and agile networking and security services.

11.3 5G and Edge Computing Integration

The convergence of SD-WAN with 5G and Edge Computing paves the way for ultra-fast, low-latency, and distributed network architectures:

- **Enhanced Connectivity:** SD-WAN combined with 5G accelerates network speeds and responsiveness, enabling new applications and use cases.

- **Edge Intelligence:** Edge Computing capabilities enhance SD-WAN's decision-making by processing data closer to the source, reducing latency and improving performance.

- **IoT Enablement:** The integration of 5G and SD-WAN supports massive Internet of Things (IoT) deployments, enabling real-time data exchange and analysis.

11.4 Evolution of SD-WAN Ecosystem

The SD-WAN ecosystem is undergoing continuous evolution, driven by technological advancements and industry collaboration:

- **Vendor Innovation:** SD-WAN vendors are continuously enhancing their solutions with new features, capabilities, and integration options.

- **Open Standards:** Industry initiatives aim to establish open standards for SD-WAN interoperability, promoting flexibility and avoiding vendor lock-in.

- **Hybrid and Multi-Cloud Integration:** SD-WAN solutions are evolving to seamlessly integrate with hybrid and multi-cloud environments, ensuring consistent connectivity and performance.

As we embark on this journey into the future of SD-WAN, the convergence of AI, SASE, 5G, Edge Computing, and the evolving SD-WAN ecosystem promises to reshape the networking landscape, unlocking new dimensions of agility, security, and innovation. With these emerging technologies on the horizon, organizations have the opportunity to harness the full potential of Software-Defined Wide Area Networking and embark on a transformative journey that redefines the boundaries of connectivity.

Chapter 12: Best Practices for SD-WAN Implementation

Implementing Software-Defined Wide Area Networking (SD-WAN) involves a strategic approach to ensure successful deployment, optimized performance, and alignment with business goals. This chapter delves into a set of best practices that organizations can follow to navigate the complexities of SD-WAN implementation. From assessing network needs and vendor selection to planning and designing the architecture, and finally, deployment, testing, and optimization, these practices serve as a guide to maximize the benefits of SD-WAN adoption.

12.1 Assessing Network Needs and Objectives

Before embarking on an SD-WAN journey, a comprehensive assessment of network needs and objectives is essential:

- **Performance Requirements:** Define performance criteria, such as latency, bandwidth, and application responsiveness, to guide SD-WAN configuration.

- **Application Prioritization:** Identify critical applications and their QoS requirements to ensure optimal performance for the most important services.

- **Scalability:** Consider future growth and scalability requirements to ensure that the SD-WAN solution can accommodate evolving network demands.

12.2 Vendor Selection and Evaluation

Selecting the right SD-WAN vendor is a crucial step that can significantly impact the success of the implementation:

- **Feature Comparison:** Evaluate vendors based on their feature sets, including security, performance optimization, analytics, and management capabilities.

- **Scalability and Flexibility:** Choose a vendor that can adapt to changing network needs and support hybrid and multi-cloud environments.

- **Interoperability:** Assess the vendor's ability to integrate with existing networking infrastructure and other technologies in your environment.

12.3 Planning and Designing SD-WAN Architecture

A well-thought-out architecture design is essential for a smooth SD-WAN implementation:

- **Topology and Deployment:** Determine the placement of SD-WAN devices, considering factors like branch locations, data centers, and cloud resources.

- **Traffic Steering Policies:** Define policies for dynamic path selection, application steering, and QoS to optimize traffic routing and performance.

- **Security Integration:** Integrate security measures such as encryption, firewall, and intrusion detection based on the organization's security requirements.

12.4 Deployment, Testing, and Optimization

The deployment phase requires careful execution, thorough testing, and ongoing optimization:

- **Phased Rollout:** Implement SD-WAN in phases, starting with a pilot deployment, to identify and address potential issues before full deployment.

- **Testing and Validation:** Rigorously test the solution's performance, security, and failover mechanisms to ensure they meet the intended objectives.

- **Ongoing Monitoring and Optimization:** Continuously monitor network performance, analyze data, and make necessary adjustments to optimize the SD-WAN environment.

By adhering to these best practices throughout the SD-WAN implementation process, organizations can streamline deployment, ensure optimal performance, and derive maximum value from their investment. As we conclude this comprehensive guide, readers are equipped with the knowledge and tools needed to embark on their SD-WAN journey, navigating the intricacies of Software-Defined Wide Area Networking with confidence and expertise.

Appendix A: Glossary of SD-WAN Terms

This glossary provides definitions for key terms and concepts related to Software-Defined Wide Area Networking (SD-WAN). It serves as a quick reference for readers to better understand the terminology used throughout the book "Mastering SD-WAN: A Comprehensive Guide to Software-Defined Wide Area Networking."

Application-Aware Routing: A feature of SD-WAN that directs network traffic based on the specific requirements and characteristics of different applications, ensuring optimal performance and user experience.

Bandwidth Aggregation: The process of combining multiple network links to increase overall bandwidth and network capacity, improving data transfer rates and responsiveness.

Cloud-Delivered SD-WAN: A deployment model where SD-WAN controllers and management components are hosted in the cloud, allowing for scalability, reduced hardware costs, and centralized management.

Dynamic Path Selection: An SD-WAN feature that dynamically selects the best path for network traffic based on real-time conditions such as latency, packet loss, and bandwidth availability.

Encryption: The process of converting data into a secure code to prevent unauthorized access during transmission, ensuring data privacy and security.

Firewall Integration: The incorporation of firewall capabilities into SD-WAN devices to filter and inspect network traffic, enhancing security by blocking unauthorized or malicious access.

Intrusion Detection and Prevention: Mechanisms within SD-WAN that identify and respond to unauthorized access attempts or malicious activities, enhancing network security.

Quality of Service (QoS): A set of techniques used in SD-WAN to prioritize and manage network traffic, ensuring that critical applications receive the necessary bandwidth and resources.

Secure Access Service Edge (SASE): An architectural framework that integrates networking and security functions into a unified cloud-based model, providing secure access for users and devices.

Traffic Shaping: The process of controlling and managing the flow of network traffic to ensure optimal performance, prevent congestion, and prioritize critical applications.

Zero-Touch Provisioning (ZTP): An automated process in SD-WAN that enables devices to be configured and deployed without manual intervention, streamlining deployment, and reducing operational complexity.

This glossary provides a concise overview of essential SD-WAN terms, supporting readers in comprehending the technical concepts discussed in the book. As you engage with the content, refer to this glossary to enhance your understanding of Software-Defined Wide Area Networking and its associated terminology.

Appendix B: SD-WAN Vendor Comparison Guide

As of my knowledge cutoff date in September 2021, there are several vendors that offer Software-Defined Wide Area Networking (SD-WAN) solutions. Keep in mind that the SD-WAN landscape may have evolved since then, and new vendors may have emerged. Here are some of the notable SD-WAN vendors up to that date:

1. Cisco (Viptela): Cisco offers SD-WAN solutions through its Viptela acquisition, providing a comprehensive SD-WAN platform with security and cloud integration.

2. VMware (VeloCloud): VMware's VeloCloud offers SD-WAN solutions with cloud-based management, security features, and application optimization.

3. Silver Peak: Silver Peak provides SD-WAN solutions with WAN optimization, security, and advanced analytics for performance monitoring.

4. Fortinet (FortiGate SD-WAN): Fortinet offers SD-WAN capabilities through its FortiGate platform, combining networking and security features.

5. Palo Alto Networks (CloudGenix): Palo Alto Networks acquired CloudGenix to enhance its SD-WAN offering, focusing on security-driven networking.

6. Riverbed: Riverbed's SD-WAN solutions emphasize performance optimization, application visibility, and cloud integration.

7. Citrix (Citrix SD-WAN): Citrix provides SD-WAN solutions that focus on application delivery, security, and user experience.

8. Aryaka: Aryaka offers a global SD-WAN platform with an emphasis on application acceleration and WAN optimization.

9. Versa Networks: Versa Networks delivers SD-WAN and SASE solutions with security and network functionality integrated into a single platform.

10. Nuage Networks: Nuage Networks, a Nokia company, offers SD-WAN and SDN solutions for data centers and enterprise networking.

11. FatPipe Networks: FatPipe Networks specializes in SD-WAN solutions with WAN optimization, load balancing, and network redundancy.

12. Masergy: Masergy provides SD-WAN solutions with integrated security, analytics, and global network connectivity.

13. Cato Networks: Cato Networks offers SD-WAN and SASE solutions designed to simplify network and security management.

14. Silverfort: Silverfort focuses on multi-cloud security and offers SD-WAN capabilities for secure connectivity.

15. CloudGenix (Cisco): Acquired by Cisco, CloudGenix provides an application-defined SD-WAN solution with an emphasis on simplicity and cloud integration.

This list is not exhaustive, and there may be other SD-WAN vendors that have emerged or gained prominence since my knowledge cutoff date. Before making any decisions, it's recommended to research the latest offerings and reviews to determine the most suitable SD-WAN vendor for your organization's needs.

Appendix C: Sample SD-WAN Policies and Configuration Templates

This appendix provides a collection of sample Software-Defined Wide Area Networking (SD-WAN) policies and configuration templates to serve as practical resources for implementing SD-WAN solutions. These templates cover various aspects of SD-WAN configuration, including traffic routing, Quality of Service (QoS) policies, security settings, and more. Feel free to adapt and customize these samples to match your organization's specific requirements.

1. Application-Aware Routing Policy:

Objective: Prioritize and route traffic based on application requirements.

```
Policy Name: Application-Aware-Routing
Applications:
  - Name: CRM-App
    Priority: High
    Path: Internet-Link

  - Name: VoIP
    Priority: Highest
    Path: MPLS-Link

  - Name: Web-Browsing
    Priority: Low
    Path: Internet-Link
```

2. QoS Policy:

Objective: Ensure optimal performance for critical applications.

```
Policy Name: QoS-Policy
Applications:
  - Name: Video-Conference
    Priority: Highest
    Bandwidth: 40%
    Loss: Low
```

```
- Name: Data-Backup
  Priority: Low
  Bandwidth: 10%
  Loss: Medium
```

3. Security Policy:

Objective: Implement firewall rules to protect the network.

```
Policy Name: Firewall-Policy
Rules:
  - Source: Guest-Network
    Destination: Internet
    Action: Allow

  - Source: Branch-Office
    Destination: Data-Center
    Action: Deny
```

4. Path Selection Policy:

Objective: Route traffic based on link quality and latency.

```
Policy Name: Path-Selection-Policy
Paths:
  - Name: MPLS-Path
    Link: MPLS-Link
    Condition: Latency < 50ms

  - Name: Internet-Path
    Link: Internet-Link
    Condition: Latency < 100ms
```

5. Zero-Touch Provisioning Template:

Objective: Configure devices for automatic deployment.

```
Device Name: Branch-Router-001
LAN Interface:
  - Name: LAN
    IP: 192.168.1.1/24
    Gateway: 192.168.1.254
```

```
WAN Interfaces:
  - Name: MPLS-Link
    IP: DHCP

  - Name: Internet-Link
    IP: DHCP
```

6. Cloud Access Policy:

Objective: Optimize cloud application performance and security.

```
Policy Name: Cloud-Access-Policy
Applications:
  - Name: Office365
    Priority: Highest
    Path: Direct-Internet-Link

  - Name: AWS-S3
    Priority: High
    Path: MPLS-Link

  - Name: Salesforce
    Priority: High
    Path: Direct-Internet-Link
```

7. Remote Office Failover Template:

Objective: Ensure seamless failover for remote office connectivity.

```
Device Name: Remote-Office-Router
LAN Interface:
  - Name: LAN
    IP: 192.168.2.1/24
    Gateway: 192.168.2.254

WAN Interfaces:
  - Name: MPLS-Link
    IP: 10.0.0.2/30

  - Name: Internet-Link
    IP: DHCP
```

8. Voice Quality Policy:

Objective: Guarantee high voice call quality for VoIP applications.

```
Policy Name: Voice-Quality-Policy
Applications:
  - Name: VoIP
    Priority: Highest
    Path: MPLS-Link
    Jitter: Low
    Latency: Low
    Loss: Low
```

9. Guest Network Isolation Policy:

Objective: Ensure guest network traffic is isolated from internal resources.

```
Policy Name: Guest-Network-Isolation
Rules:
  - Source: Guest-Network
    Destination: Internal-Network
    Action: Deny

  - Source: Guest-Network
    Destination: Internet
    Action: Allow
```

10. Hybrid Cloud Integration Policy:

Objective: Optimize traffic flow between on-premises and cloud resources.

```
Policy Name: Hybrid-Cloud-Integration
Paths:
  - Name: On-Premises-Path
    Link: MPLS-Link
    Condition: Latency < 50ms

  - Name: Cloud-Path
    Link: Direct-Internet-Link
```

```
Condition: Latency < 100ms
```

11. Security-Zone Policy:

Objective: Segregate traffic based on security requirements.

```
Policy Name: Security-Zone-Policy
Zones:
  - Name: High-Security
    Subnets: 192.168.3.0/24
    Firewall-Rules: Deny-All

  - Name: Low-Security
    Subnets: 192.168.4.0/24
    Firewall-Rules: Allow-Internet-Access
```

12. Multi-Path Load Balancing Policy:

Objective: Distribute traffic across multiple links for load balancing.

```
Policy Name: Load-Balancing-Policy
Paths:
  - Name: MPLS-Path
    Link: MPLS-Link
    Load: 50%

  - Name: Internet-Path
    Link: Internet-Link
    Load: 50%
```

Below you will find some vendor specific sample configurations.

Cisco vEdge

Configuring a Cisco vEdge SD-WAN device involves a series of steps to define policies, interfaces, routing, and security settings. Below is a simplified sample configuration for a Cisco vEdge SD-WAN device. Please note that this is a basic example, and your actual configuration may vary based on your network requirements and topology.

```
! Sample Cisco vEdge SD-WAN Configuration

system
  host-name vEdge-Router
  system-ip 192.168.1.1
  site-id 1

vpn 0
  interface ge0/0
    ip address 192.168.1.1/24
    tunnel-interface
      encapsulation ipsec
      color default

  interface ge0/1
    ip address 10.0.0.1/24
    tunnel-interface
      encapsulation ipsec
      color default

  ip route 0.0.0.0/0 192.168.1.254

policy
  route-policy Custom-Policy
    from
      color default
    then
      accept

  app-route-policy App-Policy
```

```
    from
      source 192.168.1.0/24
      to any
    then
      next-hop 10.0.0.2

security-policy
  default-action accept
  intrusion-policy basic

nhrp
  tunnel-interface ge0/0
    priority 10
  tunnel-interface ge0/1
    priority 20
```

In this example, we've configured a Cisco vEdge SD-WAN device with two interfaces (ge0/0 and ge0/1), each associated with a tunnel interface for encapsulation and IPsec. We've defined a static default route, created a custom route policy, and an application route policy for traffic steering. Additionally, basic security settings and Next Hop Resolution Protocol (NHRP) configurations have been applied.

Cisco vBond

Configuring a Cisco vBond orchestrator in an SD-WAN environment involves setting up the control plane for SD-WAN devices to establish secure connections. Here's a simplified sample configuration for a Cisco vBond SD-WAN device. Keep in mind that this is a basic example, and your actual configuration may vary based on your network requirements and topology.

```
! Sample Cisco vBond SD-WAN Configuration

system
  host-name vBond-Orchestrator
  system-ip 192.168.1.10

vbond
  interface ge0/0
    ip address 192.168.1.10/24

  organization-name MySDWANOrg
```

```
    local-system-ip 192.168.1.10

  vmanage
    organization-name MySDWANOrg
    vbond 192.168.1.10

vpn 0
  interface ge0/0
    ip address 10.0.0.1/24
    no shutdown

  ip route 0.0.0.0/0 10.0.0.254

policy
  route-policy Custom-Policy
    from
      vpn 0
    then
      accept

security-policy
  default-action accept
  intrusion-policy basic
```

In this example, we've configured a Cisco vBond SD-WAN device
with an interface (ge0/0) and defined organization and vManage
connectivity settings. We've also created a VPN interface and
applied a static default route, as well as a custom route policy and
basic security settings.

Cisco vSmart

Configuring a Cisco vSmart controller in an SD-WAN environment
involves defining policies, routes, and connectivity settings to enable
intelligent traffic steering and optimization. Here's a simplified
sample configuration for a Cisco vSmart SD-WAN controller. Keep
in mind that this is a basic example, and your actual configuration
may vary based on your network requirements and topology.

```
! Sample Cisco vSmart SD-WAN Configuration

system
  host-name vSmart-Controller
  system-ip 192.168.1.20
```

```
vpn 0
  interface ge0/0
    ip address 192.168.1.20/24

  ip route 0.0.0.0/0 192.168.1.254

vpn 1
  interface ge0/1
    ip address 10.0.1.1/24
    no shutdown

  ip route 0.0.0.0/0 10.0.1.254

policy
  route-policy Custom-Policy
    from
      color default
    then
      accept

  app-route-policy App-Policy
    from
      source 192.168.1.0/24
      to any
    then
      next-hop 10.0.1.2

security-policy
  default-action accept
  intrusion-policy basic

overlay
  tcp mss 1350
```
In this example, we've configured a Cisco vSmart SD-WAN controller with two VPN interfaces (vpn 0 and vpn 1). We've defined interfaces with IP addresses, applied static default routes, created custom route policies, an application route policy, and basic security settings. The "overlay" configuration specifies the TCP Maximum Segment Size (MSS) for optimized traffic.

Fortigate

Configuring a Fortinet SD-WAN environment involves setting up interfaces, policies, routing, and quality of service (QoS) settings to optimize traffic flow and security. Below are simplified sample configurations for a Fortinet SD-WAN deployment using the FortiGate Next-Generation Firewall platform. Please note that these are basic examples, and your actual configuration may vary based on your network requirements and topology.

1. SD-WAN Interface Configuration:

```
config system interface
    edit "SD-WAN-Link-1"
        set vdom "root"
        set ip 192.168.1.1 255.255.255.252
        set allowaccess ping https ssh http fgfm snmp
    next
end
```

2. SD-WAN Zone Configuration:

```
config system zone
    edit SD-WAN
        set interface "SD-WAN-Link-1" "SD-WAN-Link-2"
# Add relevant interfaces
    next
end
```

3. SD-WAN Rule Configuration:

```
config firewall policy
    edit 1
        set srcintf "internal"
        set dstintf "SD-WAN"
        set srcaddr "user subnet"
        set dstaddr "web server address"
        set action accept
        set schedule "always"
        set service "allowed services"
        set sdwan-rule "SD-WAN-Rule-1"
    next
end
```

4. SD-WAN Rule Configuration with QoS:

```
config firewall policy
    edit 2
        set srcintf "internal"
        set dstintf "SD-WAN"
        set srcaddr "voice subnet"
        set dstaddr "voice server address"
        set action accept
        set schedule "always"
        set service "voice services"
        set sdwan-rule "SD-WAN-Rule-2"
        set traffic-shaper "QoS-Profile"
    next
end
```

5. SD-WAN Interface Load Balancing Configuration:

```
config system sdwan-interface
    edit "SD-WAN-Rule-1"
        set load-balance simple
        set interface "SD-WAN-Link-1" "SD-WAN-Link-2"
# Add relevant interfaces
        set member "SD-WAN-Link-1" weight 50
        set member "SD-WAN-Link-2" weight 50
    next
end
```

Please note that these sample policies and templates are provided for illustrative purposes only. These sample SD-WAN policies and configuration templates cover a range of scenarios and use cases, including cloud access optimization, remote office failover, voice quality assurance, security isolation, hybrid cloud integration, security zones, and load balancing. As always, ensure that you customize and validate these templates to align with your organization's specific requirements and network architecture. By leveraging these templates, you can expedite your SD-WAN implementation while adhering to best practices and achieving desired outcomes. They may need to be adapted and customized to suit your organization's specific network architecture, applications, and requirements. Always thoroughly test and validate configurations before deploying them in a production environment. Use these resources as a starting point to expedite your SD-WAN implementation while ensuring alignment with your organization's needs and best practices.

Index

T

U

V

W

"Mastering SD-WAN: A Comprehensive Guide to Software-Defined Wide Area Networking" is a thorough exploration of SD-WAN technology, designed to equip network professionals, IT managers, and decision-makers with the knowledge and tools needed to harness the power of software-defined networking in wide area environments. From fundamental concepts to real-world case studies, this book serves as a definitive resource for understanding, implementing, and optimizing SD-WAN solutions. With a focus on practical insights and best practices, readers will gain the expertise to transform their network infrastructure and elevate their organization's connectivity capabilities into the future.

Printed in Great Britain
by Amazon

40561185R00036